Paris Houses

Paris Houses

Edited by:
Maria Cristina Fregni

Motta

Edited and published by
24 ORE Motta Cultura srl, Milan

Editing: Anna Mainoli

Translation: Nella Burnett-Stuart

Cover
Lazzarini Pickering Architetti
Apartment in Avenue of New York
Paris 2008
Photo: Matteo Piazza, Milan

First edition
April 2009

ISBN: 978-88-6413-015-6

Printed in Italy

Contents

Who has never thought, at least once in their lives, to abandon everything and go to live in an attic in Paris?

The French capital has always held a particular charm for all those who come in contact with its mix of bohemian atmosphere and sumptuousness.

It is not that simple to trace the reasons for such a level of appeal. Writers, poets and ordinary people are always trying to define the spirit of this city. Paris is so alive and vivid in our imagination because of numerous films and novels set there, that it almost risks becoming a non- place.

Paris forms a fascinating world far from everyday routine. It is so original and elegant that it makes the capital of France the city of dreams where everybody wants to live. Hemingway, who lived there in his youth when training to be a journalist, defined Paris as "a moveable feast".

A city so lively and stimulating from a cultural and aesthetic point of view to be the ideal place for those who want to hide away in its narrow streets in search of inspiration or for those who want to show off by emerging themselves in the sparkling and elegant luxury of the *boulevards.*

Paris is a continually evolving city, always keeping up with the times, and able to renew itself like few other cities in Europe. It is a very important architectural centre stimulated by international talent that finds the ideal conditions in which to grow and develop.

Between major urban and social revolutions

Paris has always faced ,with decisiveness
and certainty, the problems that have presented
themselves, often with convincing and original
results. This has been thanks to many different
people - politicians, city planners, artists -
who have believed in the link between the form
and function of the city and in the capacity
of the urban structure to renew itself without
losing its identity.
Without going too far back in time we merely need
to look at the last decade to understand what
we are talking about : the image of Paris is linked
to the great names of architecture like Piano
and Rogers, Gae Aulenti, Jean Nouvel and I.M.
Pei as well as important politicians like Pompidou,
Giscard d'Estaing and Mitterand who have been
supporters and patrons of projects, sometimes
grandiose; certainly capable of changing the
face of entire areas of the city.

Apart from important buildings there are also
examples of urban redevelopment such as the
Villette project and the Andre Citroen Park.
All these projects are just the 'tip of the iceberg' :
the history of recent architecture in Paris is full
of numerous minor interventions to residential
buildings worthy of the "ville lumière" that we
all love.
Behind an apparent immutability Paris is a city
that knows how to move in time and in space,
how to transform and generate new fashions
whilst remaining faithful to itself.
Even if the historically prestigious areas are

by now consolidated – Champs Elysées,
Trocadéro, Saint Germain des Prés, Opera and
Marais with the l'Ile Saint Louis – every three
or four years an area, up until that moment
of less importance, has the capacity to reinvent
itself and become fashionable; dominating the city
scene and generating one after the other building
redevelopments, new buildings and substantial
property development.

The most recent case is the Bastille district which
in five years has become the trendiest of the
French capital. A historic quarter of Paris,
a symbol of the revolution, up until a few years
ago the Bastille district was not considered
a popular shopping area of international repute
by the French. Things have now changed
radically: interesting boutiques and art galleries
have sprung up around Rue de Charonne
and Rue Keller together with meeting places
for the young and so called "creative class".
'Charonne District – as it has been renamed –
is a cosmopolitan, trendy and alternative village,
famous but still underground", explains Clarent,
one of the creators of the rebirth. It is a bit like
Nolita and Lower East Side in New York or the
streets of Portobello in London, with fashionable
shops but with an added touch of typically
Parisian class.

If you want to find the new bohemian Paris
you need to go to the area of Belleville and
Ménilmontant where, day and night, there are
all kinds of artistic and social events going on.

This old working class district, where Edith Piaf was born in 1915, has always been somewhere Parisians have gone to breathe in the 'country air' ; added to this particular feature it has, for sometime now, become a meeting place for immigrants from North Africa and China. It is currently one of the favourites places for the so called radical chic. Due to this variety of characteristics numerous artists have their studios here and this contributes to the myriad of meeting places with a bohemian atmosphere.

In Paris even projects relating to major public works are treated as an opportunity to renew entire areas of the city. For example, the Stadium of France in Saint Tennis: the realisation of this project has in fact laid the foundations for the redevelopment of the northwest district of Paris – Montmartre, Barbeés, Saint-Ouen, Saint Denis – where up until fairly recently few Parisians would have considered going to. The redevelopment project in progress has given new life to the traditional nature of the Butte. Today there is a metropolitan feel that attracts younger residents who often come from the world of culture and the creative arts.

Near districts like this, of recent redevelopment, are those areas of the city which have always been considered the most desirable as they are very chic and have the *grandeur* typical of the French capital.

The Marais, for example, was the quarter of the old markets where the Jewish community lived.

There are still a lot of food shops but the majority have been transformed into high class delicatessens. Alongside these have appeared fashionable bars, shops of vintage clothes, furnishing and design. The Marais is frequented by both Parisians and tourists alike and has a central position in the geography and history of Paris : all one needs to do is take a stroll in the streets of the district in the early hours of Sunday morning to have tangible proof of its vitality. The lower half of the district leads in design and fashion and the upper half, near the Picasso Museum, is going through a process of modernisation : the restructuring of buildings is the order of the day and innovative and beautiful living spaces are being created. In the lively quarter of Saint Germain de Prés on the so-called Left Bank, the brightly lit shop windows of designer boutiques mix with those of the Café de Flore, the Brasserie Lipp and Les Deux Magots which, in the seventies, were frequented by Sartre and are now the choice of students and young intellectuals; here there are apartments of great prestige that offer breathtaking views of the tree lined boulevards of the city and are quite possibly furnished by one of the more noted Parisian interior designers like Alberto Pino.

In the north western suburbs of Paris, beyond L'Arc di Triomphe, is Défense which is the most modern and high tech area of the city. This area is a must for all who love architecture and design and there is a concentration of skyscrapers with ample pedestrian zones and the biggest shopping centre in Europe, Les Quatre Temps, where you can find everything, buy anything and eat anything. It has only recently become a residential area which is attracting professionals and families because of its infrastructure and services.

We can see that each area of Paris has its own character that is often reflected in the houses found there. The planning of the majority of Parisian houses plays with elements common to every area of the city like the characteristic light from the sky that reflects on the mainly light colours of the buildings, the *divertissement* of the maze of courtyards, gardens, stairways, dormer windows, sloping roofs, the intriguing peek-a-boo skylights, of *bistrot* and *brasseries* along the streets, long walks along the many kilometres of boulevards, apartments and designer houses elaborating in their own way the spirit of the district they are in and becoming an integral part of its identity.

We have the elegant and luxurious apartments that are representative of the centre, the lofts, sometimes attached to artists studios along the Seine, the colourful bohemian apartments of Montmartre and the new trendy areas and polyfunctional one bedroomed flats of the working class neighbourhoods.

Whether we are talking about the project of a well known architect or from a new studio one thing we can be certain about is that this city is not

frightened of taking risks. Paris is a many-sided, dynamic, lively and always scintillating city that is capable of maintaining its past without losing sight of the future and which offers its inhabitants a stage and a place to live without equal.
''Paris Never Ends" is the title of the book by the Spanish writer Enrique Vila Matas. And the never-ending evolvement of its houses fully demonstrates this fully.

Maria Cristina Fregni

Paris Houses

16

Loft in Montmartre
2009

2design

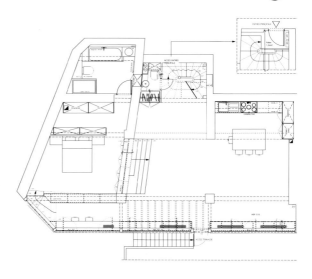

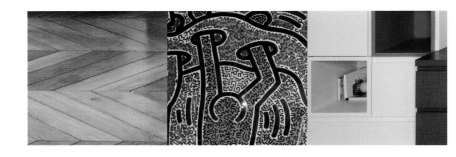

26

The design of made to measure
elements for a Parisian apartment
2008

Agnès & Agnès Architecture

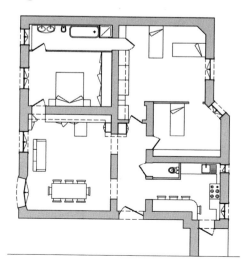

34

Ecological Loft
2007

Atelier D

44

House Conversion
and Courtyard layout
2003

belus & hénocq architectes

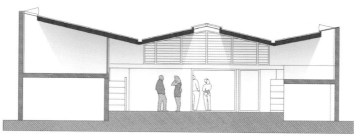

Conversion of a music shop
into an apartment
2005

BOX

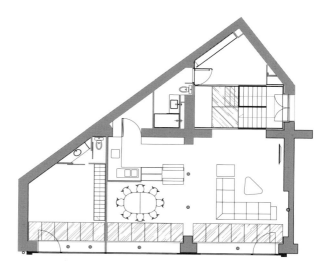

64

Saint Maur Flat
2005

Cheikh-Djavadi

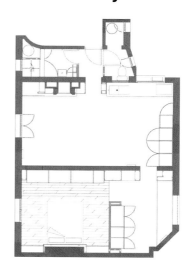

74

Apartment C&T
2004

fabienne couvert
& guillaume terver architectes

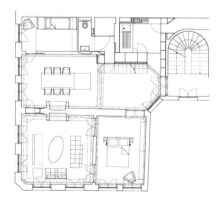

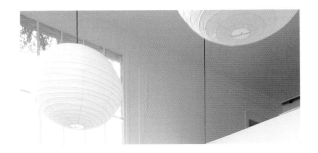

84

fabienne couvert
& guillaume terver architectes

96

The antiloft
2005

doray - wra

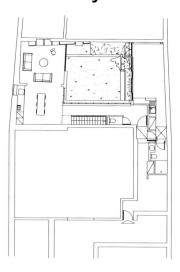

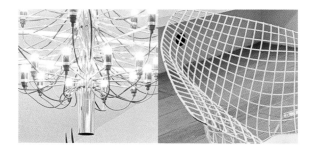

106

FREDERIC HAESEVOETS
ARCHITECTE

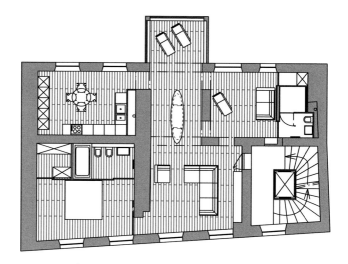

116

FREDERIC HAESEVOETS
ARCHITECTE

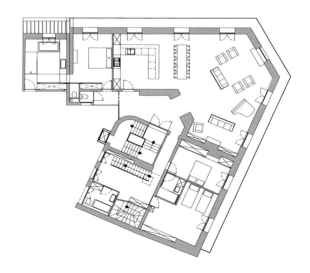

128

FREDERIC HAESEVOETS
ARCHITECTE

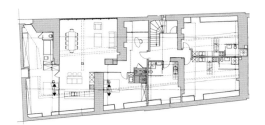

140

CK06
2009

Pablo Katz Architecte
(GPK ARCHITECTURE)

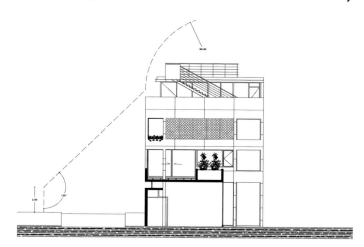

154

Loft Paris
2007

Landmark Architecture

170

Apartment in Avenue of New York
2008

lazzarini pickering architetti

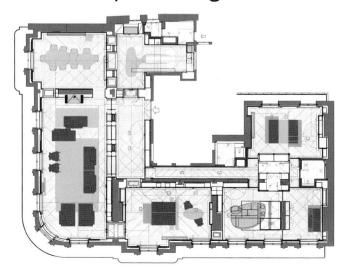

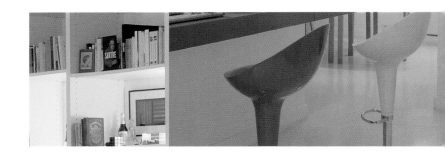

182

karin leopold
et françois fauconnet

Olympische Spiele München 1972

194

Malesherbes
2007

karin leopold
et françois fauconnet

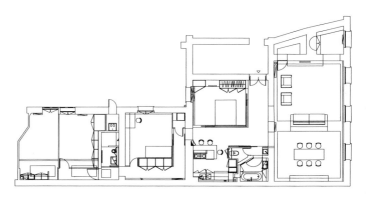

204

Loft rue de Savoie
1998

Littow Architects

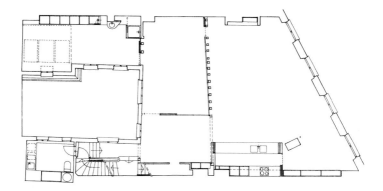

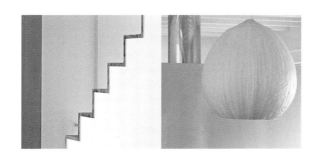

214

Loft avenue du Maine
2004

Littow Architects

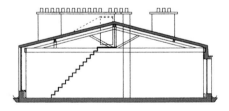

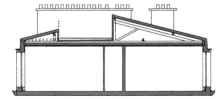

226

Loft rue de l'Ouest
2006

Littow Architects

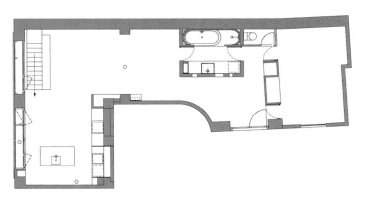

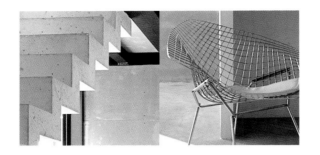

234

MK/3-VA, villa atelier
2002

METEK

246

MK/22-SP, loft in the Marais
2006

METEK

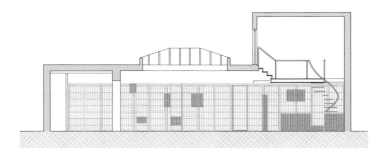

254

MK/55-TR
2007

METEK

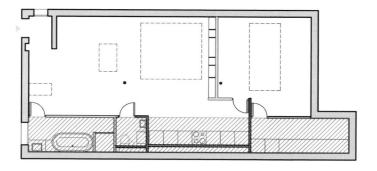

Walking up
through gat
had passe
streets, ca
flower sta
sidewalks
strange   r
walled villa
the light
increased as
top, with de
to the e
of it, thror
a   peace
rose from

262

**MK/17-AR, The conversion
of two apartments
into a two storey apartment
2008**

METEK

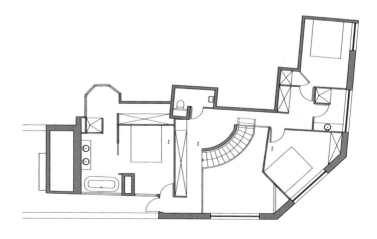

270

Maison A
2006

Moussafir,
Denoyel, Wuilmot

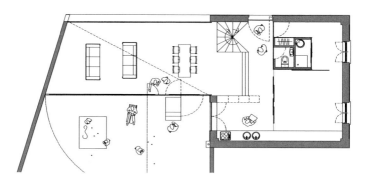

282

Maison Dubesset
2006

OTAA

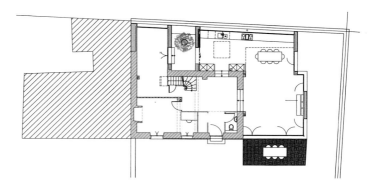

294

Val-de-Grâce
2007

christian pottgiesser
architecturespossibles

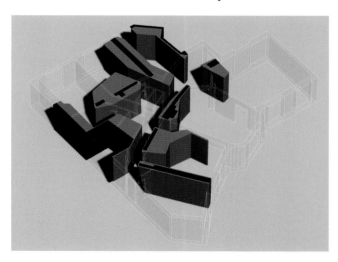

306

PoP
2007

Cyril Rheims /Ki architecture

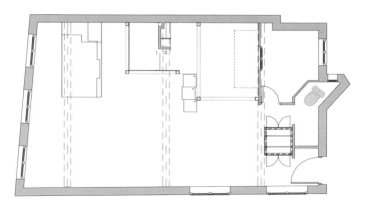

316

The Conversion of an artist's
studio into an office and home
2005

Philippe Roussel Architecte

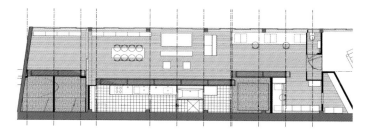

330

House Rubix
2008

Salama

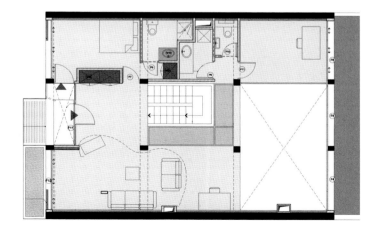

342

Apartment A
2007

Carl Fredrik Svenstedt

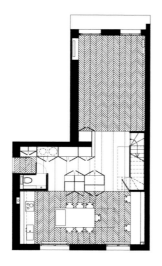

356

Loft 19
2007

Veillon Architecture

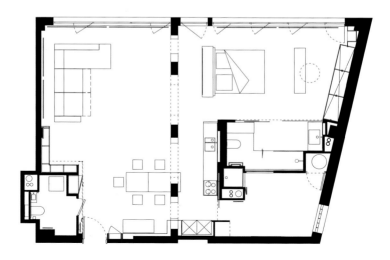

Loft R
2007

Veillon Architecture

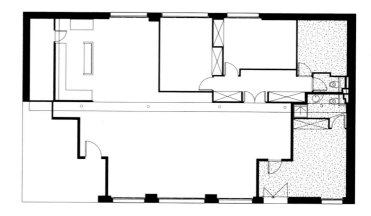

biographies

2design:

www.2designarchitecture.com
Christopher Charveriat graduated from Camondo in Paris and Delphine Martin-Michaud from Kingston University in London. Together they founded 2design, an interior design studio, in 2003. They have completed numerous projects in France (lofts and apartments in Paris and prestigious villas in the South of the country) and the rest of the world. Amongst the projects of the studio are a private club in Bogotà, the house of the footballer Eric Cantona in Brittany, boutiques in London, and the setting up of an exhibition in Ile Maurice. www.2designarchitecture.com

project at page 16
Loft in Montmartre
2009
collaborator: Jean-Baptiste Leroux
photographer: Jean-Baptiste Leroux

Agnès & Agnès Architecture

Agnès Guillemin and Agnès Chryssostalis were born in 1976 and graduated in Architecture from the Paris-La Seine school in 2001. They founded Agnès and Agnès Architecture in 2005 after having collaborated with different architects studios such as Christian de Portzamparc, ADC Parallèles, Rechen & Robert and Valode & Pistre. In 2007 after numerous assignments they founded Agnès and Agnès Design that completed the initial set up of the studio. Agnès and Agnès operate on different levels, from urban planning to furniture design, and collaborate closely with everybody involved in a project. Amongst their recent projects are a restaurant in Brussels, the extension of a house in Paris and offices for Baccarat in Paris.
www.agnesetagnes.com

project at page 26
The design of made to measure elements for a Parisian apartment
2008
photographer: Bertrand Limbour

Atelier D

Atelier D is an organisation that brings together three architects – Vanessa Grob (Conception, Chile, 1972), Mattias Piani (Rome, 1972, Ilhem Belhatem (Algiers 1966) – all with the same objective : the creation and carrying out of a new sustainable architecture that respects the human, social and natural environment. They have completed projects for the private and public sectors and for the industrial sector.Their intention was to improve each time the quality of the buildings and that of the comfort of the clients as an integral part of the project. They were awarded third prize for the competition *Lo sguardo del architetto su Biella,* 2008; they developed the project for the OPAC collective residences, Paris 2008; they took part in the Agora 2008 competition with the Dense Cité project.
www.atelier-d.fr

project at page 34
Ecological Loft
2007
photographer: Nicolas Heintz

belus & hénocq architectes

Guillaume Belus and Adrien Hénocq are long standing friends who, over the years, have developed a business that involves different aspects of planning, from urban to landscape architecture. Belus and Hénocq graduated from the School of Architecture in Paris-Tolbiac where they founded the collective Atelier Excelsior that won the Tony Garnier prize for urban planning in 1998. Adrien Héncoq also took up teaching: between 1999 and 2004 he supported Sébastien Marot, Stéphane Hirschberger and Georges Descombes during the course they held at the University of Marne-la- Valle. The studio of Belus & Hénocq Architects opened in 2008 to cement a long collaboration and after a short time, still in 2008, they won second prize at the Salon Bois d'Angers in the category Habitat Groupé. Projects completed by the two architects that deserve mention are the residential complexes in Mormant (2008), a series of terraced houses in Thouaré-sur-Loire (2008), the PLAI/PLUS houses in Cergy Pontoise (2006) and the forty units of the Asnières complex (2002). Public buildings include a cultural centre in Rochecorbon (2000) and the Loges du Zenith in Paris (2008), while the urban projects include an important park at Maison-Alfort (2003) and the layout of the area south of Amiens (2001).
www.architectes.org/portfolios/belus-henocq-architectes

project at page 44
House Conversion and Court layout
2003
photographer: Raphael Chipault
Raphaël Chipault

BOX : Agnés Plumet and Bertrand Toussaint

Agnés Plumet and Bertrand Toussaint founded the Architect's Studio Box in Paris in 2001. Agnés Plumet was born in 1971 and graduated from the School of Architecture of Paris-Villemin in 2000. She has collaborated with various Parisian architects studios, amongst which Jean-Marc Ibos and Myrto Plumet (*Palazzo delle Belle arti* of Lille, the Rescue Centre in Nanterre), Marc Mimram Ingénierie and Brunet-Saunier Architecture.
Bertrand Toussaint, born in 1969, was trained as a cabinet maker and then as an interior designer. He collaborated with Jean Nouvel (the courthouse of Nantes) before joining the studio RFR that specialised in the finishing of the outer membrane of buildings. He is currently the director of RFR and collaborates with architects like Renzo Piano, Jean Nouvel and Toyo Ito.

project at page 52
Conversion of a music shop into an apartment
2005
photograper: © Alain Potignon / Phuong Pfeufer

Cheikh-Djavadi

Cheikh-Djavadi, of Iranian origin, was born in 1959 and studied architecture at Paris Art School. His projects were published in "AD" (French and Spanish editions), IDEAT 2008, 'Arquitectura y Diseño', 25 Beautiful Homes 2008. Amongst his completed projects are some villas in Ibiza and a swimming pool and ice skating rink in Chartres.

project at page 64
Saint Maur Flat
2005
photographer: © Alain Potignon / Phuong Pfeufer

fabienne couvert & guillaume terver architectes

Fabienne Couvert graduated from the School of Architecture in Grenoble in 1990. Thanks to a grant from the Villa Medici prize he lived in Rome from 1994-1995. In 1998 he conducted a research project on traffic flow in the United States for which he won the Delano Aldrich prize.

Guillaume Terver has lived in Rome since 1987. In 1993 he was one of the best graduates at the School of Graphic Arts and Interior Design in Paris. In 2000 he won the Met de Penninghen prize. Since 1993 he has taught Interior Design at the School of Graphic Arts and Design.

In 1998 the studio won the Moniteur group prize for best project and in 2001 he received the nomination for the first Palmarès of Réhabilitation of the French Ministry of Culture.
cxtarchitecture.com

projects at page 74, 84
Apartment C&T
2004
collaborators: Cristina Ayesa Ruiz
photographers: Guillaume Terver

House DL&B
2005
collaborators: Cristina Ayesa Ruiz
photographer: Guillaume Terver

doray – wra

Vladimir Doray graduated in architecture in 2002 and has had his own studio WRA since 2004. This studio manages a small number of projects that are developed on a mult imodal approach; Doray works with Hélène Michelson who looks after the sustainable development and a number of professionals from different sectors who, although leaving Doray with the responsibility of the majority of projects,contribute with a variety of skills, energy and new ideas. In 2008 Doray was awarded *Les Noveaux Albums des Jeunes Architectes*, a recognition conferred by the French Minister of Culture not just for the quality of the projects realised but also for the innovative approach that characterises the activity of the studio.
www.wildrabbits.fr

project at page 96
The antiloft
2005
collaborator: Hélène Michelson
photography: Bertrand Limbour

frederic haesevoets architects

Frédéric Haesevoets was born in 1977 and graduated in architecture at Lambert Lombard (Liège) in 2000. He lives and works in Brussels. He has participated in a number of competitions at the Universal Arts Centre, New York 2005 ; the New City and Contemporary Art Museum in South Africa, 2007; Headquarters Velux Belgium, 2008. He has worked on restaurants, hotels and apartments in Paris, Istanbul, Brussels and Cannes. His projects have been exhibited in Pittsburgh, New York, Liege and Cape Town.
www.frederic-haesevoets.com

project at page 106, 116, 128
JPR001
2006
photographer: Christophe Haesevoets

LR001
2006
photographer: Christophe Haesevoets

ST001
2007
photographer: Christophe Haesevoets

Pablo KATZ

Pablo Katz studied at the Faculty of Architecture and Urbanism of Buenos Aires and the School of Architecture in Paris-Belleville. After years of practice in studios in Argentina, Brazil and France Pablo Katz founded GPK Architecture and then Pablo KATZ ARCHITECTURE. He has designed the Departmental Centre for Communication in the Dordogne, the restructuring of a 15th century building for L'Opéra du Rhin in Strasbourg.

He has taught at the School of Architecture in Paris and at the Academy of Arts in Stuttgart. He has represented Europe as a town planner at the Argentinian committee of architecture and town planning. Pablo Katz is also president of the French Society of Architects.

www.pablokatz-architecture.com

project at page 40
CK06
2009
collaborators: Julius Cesnulevicius (planning) e Vladimir Doray (building site)
photographer: Arnaud Rinuccini

Landmark Architecture

Alban Flipo was born in 1966 and graduated in 1991 at the La Seine School of Architecture in Paris.

After working for Cartier International as director of the architecture department he founded Landmark Architecture in 1998, specializing in identity and brand projects in the luxury sector (Van Cleef and Arpels, Balenciaga, Jaeger Lecoultre, JM Weston).

www.landmark-architecture.fr

project at page 154
Loft Paris
2007
photographer: Jérôme Galland / Aleph

lazzarini pickering architetti

Claudio Lazzaroni was born in Rome in 1953 and graduated from the University La Sapienza. Carl Pickering was born in Sydney in 1960 and after moving to Italy in 1980 graduated in architecture from the University of Venice. In 1983 they founded the studio Lazzarini Pickering in Rome which is active in different areas of planning : industrial design, interiors, restructuring, nautical design and gardens. Recent projects include the development of the worldwide brand image of Fendi, the restructuring of Palazzo Boncompagni in Rome as well as offices and showroom for the Fendi Group, the restructuring of "Il Messagero" offices in Rome, the restoration of an existing building and a project for a new building in the historical centre of Prague, two villas at Cap Ferrat and one at Villefranche in France. In the area of nautical design the Wally B and Wallypower boats. The studio has received numerous awards of international prestige.
www.lazzarinipickering.com

project at page 170
Apartment in Avenue of New York
2008
collaborators: Barbara Fragala, Alessandra Belia
photographe: Matteo Piazza

karin leopold
et françois fauconnet

Karin Leopold and Francois Fauconnet founded the studio of the same name in 1987 with the head office in Paris. They both graduated in architecture in Paris in 1982 and 1983 respectively. Karin Leopold has taught at the ESAM in Paris since 2000 and Francois Fauconnet at the EPSAAVP in Paris -La - Villette since 1992. The studio mainly operates in the field of residential building and interior planning. Recent projects to highlight are : the upgrading and the extension of a house in Herblay, 2007; a building of four floors in Paris, 2007 ; 22 houses in Saint Sorlin d'Arves and 20 in Viroflay, 2007; the raising of a building for offices in Boulogne, in process of realisation.
www.leopold-fauconnet.com

projects at pages 182, 194
Pyramides
2006
collaborators: Grégoire De la Forest, Virginie Carthagena
photographer: © Cécile Septet / Phuong Pfeufer

Malesherbes
2007
collaborators: Lucy Phillips, Remi Knep
photographer: © Cécile Septet / Phuong Pfeufer

Littow Architects

Pekka Littow was born in Oulu, Finland in 1959. In 1958 he was awarded a diploma from the School of Architecture in the same town. He continued his studies at the School of Architecture in Versailles and then he graduated at the Istitute of Architecture in Paris, with a specialisation in constructions in concrete.
The second member of Littow Architects is Sophie Cabanes. Born in Paris in 1960 she graduated from the Paris La Seine School of Architecture in 1985. She obtained a second diploma at the Art School of Fontainebleu in 1988. Between 1988 and 1989 she attended the department of interior design at the School of Industrial art in Helsinki.
The studio works on commercial and office buildings, public buildings, houses, restructuring and furniture design and exhibition lay out.
www.littowarchitectes.com

projects at page 204, 214, 226
Loft rue de Savoie
1998
photographer: Pekka Littow

Loft rue avenue du Maine
2004
photographer: Pekka Littow

Loft de l'Ouest
2006
photographer: Pekka Littow

METEK, Sarah Bitter
& Nathalie Blaise
architectes

The architects studio Metek was founded in 2001 in New York and then moved to Paris in 2004. The studio has its main office in the first project built by Metek : a studio house in Belleville. This project, which is highly thought of, was chosen for the 2004 *Prix of Gran public de l'architecture* . awarded by the French Ministry of Culture and is permanently displayed at the Arsenal Pavilion. Sarah Bitter manages the studio founded together with Nathalie Blaise. She graduated from the Versailles school of architecture, and has studied and worked in Marseilles, Barcelona, Seville, and Berlin. She teaches at different architecture schools amongst which the Marne la Vallée.
Amongst the projects completed by Metek are the Tourist Information Centre of Fréjus, eight eco sustainable apartments in Paris and a set design for the 2008 Living Architects Festival of Montpellier in 2008.
www.metek-architecture.com

projects at pages 234, 246, 254, 262
MK/3-VA, villa atelier
2002
photographer: Joël Cariou

MK/22-SP, loft in Marais
2006
photographer: Bertrand Limbour

MK/55-TR
2007
photographer: Bertrand Limbour

MK/17-AR, Conversion of two apartments into a two-storey apartment
2008
photographer: MOPA

Moussafir, Denoyel, Wuilmot

Jacques Moussafir was born in 1957 and graduated in architecture in 1993 at the Paris-Tolbiac Architects School. He has taken part in numerous competitions, amongst which the one the Museum of Quai Brandy with MVRDV and Périphériques. He was responsible for the restructuring of the library at the Paris-Saint Denis University. He is currently studying the reconversion of the Henry IV area in the Castle of Fontainebleu into the European Centre of Chamber Music, a programme of collective housing in Paris and a hotel complex in Mozambique. In 2001 Moussafir was nominated for the Equerre d'Argent del "Moniteur" Award with the UFR Arts di Saint-Denis project and was mentioned for the AR+D awards.

isabell Denoyel was born in 1960 and graduated in 1987 at the Paris-Villemin School of Architecture. She collaborates with various architects studios concentrating in particular on the restructuring of hospitals, houses and office tower blocks. This experience has allowed her to develop a strong awareness of working on existing structures.

Eric Wuilmot was born in Belgium in 1959 and graduated at the Tournai School of Architecture. His projects range from the restructuring of apartments to the layout of lofts, from the extension of pavillions to the construction of new accomodation. He is currently working on a hotel extension, a house in the centre of Paris and a hotel on the cliffs of Bandiagara in Sangha in Mali.
www.moussafir.fr

project at page 270
Maison A
2006
photographer: © Alain Potignon / Phuong Pfeufer

OTAA – Agence d'Architecture Olivier Thin

Olivier Thin was born in 1966 in Neuilly-sur-Seine. In 1993 he graduated from the Paris-la-Seine School of Architecture and in 1994 he did a Masters in Architecture and Urban planning at the University of Pennsylvania. In 1998 he founded the OTAA studio. Amongst the projects recently completed are the restructuring of an apartment, the elevation of a *hotel particulier* (Paris XVI) and an office building in Paris VIII. In progress is the Ciad Embassy, a complex of 35 residences and shops, both in Paris, as well as 11 appartments in Boulogne-Billancourt.
www.otaa.fr

projects at page 282

Maison Dubesset
2006
collaborators: Dimitri Leduc (interior design)
photographers: © Alain Potignon / Phuong Pfeufer

christian pottgiesser architecturespossibles

Christian Pottgiesser was born in Germany in 1965. He graduated from the Paris-Villemin School of Architecture and then followed a course of philosophy studies at the Paris 1- Panthèon Sorbonne University. In 1991 he founded his own studio which from 2005 took the name of Christian Pottgeisser Architecturepossibiles. Amongst the awards received are the Contractworld Award in 2008 and the AIT Best of Office Architecture Award, 2008. Recently completed projects are the offices at Huot and Pons in Paris (2006) and the installation of the festival of Chaumont sur Loire (2006).
pottgiesser.free.fr

projects at page 294
Val-de-Grâce
2007
collaborators: Pascale Pottgiesser (artist), Alejandro Ratier (designer), Matthieu Lott (architect)
photographer: Hervé Abbadie

Cyril Rheims /Ki architecture

Cyril Rheims was born in 1971 and graduated from the Montpellier School of Architecture in 2000. In 2004 he founded the Ki architecture studio. He loves planning in collaboration with his clients, achieving an assertive and colourful architecture and with the simple aim of the well being of his customers. He has carried out the renovation of apartments, new constructions, extensions, shops and design of fittings.
www.cyrilrheims.com

project at page 306
PoP
2007
photographer: Hervé Abbadie

Philippe Roussel Architecte - Ph. Roussel & C. Kalus Architectes

Philippe Roussel was born in Avignon in 1964 and graduated from the Marseille- Luminy School of architecture. Before opening her own studio in 1998 Roussel worked for a number of years in the Francois Deslaugiers studio as project coordinater and collaborated with other important studios like ADP, Paul Audreu and Franck Hammouténe. Since 2000 he has taught at the Marseilles School of architecture.
Christine Kalus was born in 1971 in Créteil (Ile-de-France) and after having attended the Arts and Crafts conservatory in Paris she graduated in architecture from the School of Paris-la-Villete-UP6. Up until 1998 she collaborated with some important artists studios like Francois Deslaugiers and ADP.
Recent completed projects by Roussel that are worth mentioning are a theatre hall with 600 seats in Saint-Cyprien, a villa at Noisy-le-Grand, the restructuring of a theatre at Boulogne-Billancourt, two pedestrian walkways at the exhibition Park at Paris-Nord-Le Bourget, the media library and executive offices at the Action Culturelle in Montgeron, the music school and amphitheatre for the community of Grand Rodez and the all-purpose centre at Manosque. Projects of the studio have appeared in various publications like "Le Moniteur", "Maison Magazine", and " Architectures à vivre".

project at page 316
Conversion of an artist's studio into an office and home
2005
photographer: © Cécile Septet / Phuong Pfeufer

salama

Frank Salma was born in 1967 and graduated at the Paris-Belleville School of Architecture in Paris. Since 2004 he has taught design at the special School of architecture and over the years has written numerous articles on Japanese architecture for magazines like "Techniques and Architecture", "Beaux Arts", and "Casabella". Amongst his projects – overall more than 100 houses – those that stand out are the houses near and in the centre of Paris and those in Lille and Châtillon. His work has been published in architecture and furniture design magazines like "Archi Cree, "D'A", "Le Moniteur", "Casa Viva", and books that include his projects are *Houses International*, *Guide of Modern Architecture in Paris* and *Paris Projects*.
www.frank-salama.fr

project at page 330
Hous Rubix
2008
photographer: Hervé Abbadie

Carl Fredrik Svenstedt

Carl Fredik Svenstedt was born in Stockholm in 1967 and studied at Harvard University and Yale School of Architecture. He is Associate Professor at the special School of Architecture in Paris and his studio is also in the French capital. Amongst projects he has completed are a prefabricated residential complex in wood for students in Compiègne; Villa S; Take Home House, a barn conversion ; the offices of the Swedish Chamber of Commerce in paris, inaugurated by His majesty the King of Sweden. His work is published in the "Wallpaper Design Directory", "Architecture Review" and "Frame".
carlfredriksvenstedt.com

project at page 342
Apartment A
2007
photographer: Hervé Abbadie

Veillon Architecture

Odile Veillon was born in 1965. After having attended the Bordeaux School of Architecture for two years he decided to pursue his studies with Henri Ciriani in Paris. He was awarded his diploma in architecture in 1994 and then he realised his dream by doing a course in fashion design until 1997. In 2000 he opened his own architecture studio, concentrating on restructuring and the private sector.

projects at page 356, 366

Loft 19
2007
photographer: © Alain Potignon / Phuong Pfeufer

Loft R
1999
photographer: Bertrand Limbour

Photographic references

Hervé Abbadie, Paris
Joël Cariou, Paris
Raphaël Chipault, Paris
Jérôme Galland / Aleph, Paris
Christophe Haesevoets, Bruxelles
Nicolas Heintz, Paris
Jean-Baptiste Leroux, Paris
Bertrand Limbour, Paris
Pekka Littow, Paris
MOPA, Paris
Matteo Piazza, Milan
© Alain Potignon, Parigi / Phuong Pfeufer, Paris
Arnaud Rinuccini, Paris
© Cécile Septet, Parigi / Phuong Pfeufer, Paris
Guillaume Terver, Paris

The publisher is available for any queries
regarding pictures that have not been accredited.